NEW ENGLAND

PATRIOTS

BY JOSH ANDERSON

Stride
An Imprint of The Child's World®
childsworld.com

The Child's World
childsworld.com

Published by The Child's World®
800-599-READ • www.childsworld.com

Photography Credits
Cover: © Maddie Meyer / Staff / Getty Images; page 1: © Africa Studio / Shutterstock; page 3: © Maddie Meyer / Staff / Getty Images; page 5: © Maddie Meyer / Staff / Getty Images; page 6: © George Rose / Stringer / Getty Images; page 9: © Al Bello / Staff / Getty Images; page 10: © Adam Glanzman / Stringer / Getty Images; page 11: © stevezmina1 / Getty Images; page 12: © Maddie Meyer / Staff / Getty Images; page 12: © Kevin C. Cox / Staff / Getty Images; page 13: © Mike Kullen / Associated Press; page 13: © Jim Rogash / Stringer / Getty Images; page 14: © Elsa / Staff / Getty Images; page 15: © Mike Ehrmann / Staff / Getty Images; page 16: © Bob Levey / Stringer / Getty Images; page 16: © TSN/Icon SMI / Newscom; page 17: © Doug Pensinger / Staff / Getty Images; page 17: © Icon SMI / Newscom; page 18: © Staff / Getty Images; page 18: © Brian Bahr / Staff / Getty Images; page 19: © Brian Bahr / Staff / Getty Images; page 19: © Al Bello / Staff / Getty Images; page 20: © Maddie Meyer / Staff / Getty Images; page 20: © Elsa / Staff / Getty Images; page 21: © Chris Trotman / Stringer / Getty Images; page 21: © Grant Halverson / Stringer / Getty Images; page 22: © Maddie Meyer / Staff / Getty Images; page 23: © Adam Glanzman / Stringer / Getty Images; page 23: © stevezmina1 / Getty Images; page 25: © Maddie Meyer / Staff / Getty Images; page 26: © Rob Carr / Staff / Getty Images; page 29: © Eliot J. Schechter / Stringer / Getty Images

ISBN Information
9781503857650 (Reinforced Library Binding)
9781503860582 (Portable Document Format)
9781503861947 (Online Multi-user eBook)
9781503863309 (Electronic Publication)

LCCN 2021952634

Printed in the United States of America

BRINGING THE WORLD TO YOUNG READERS 1968

TABLE OF CONTENTS

GO PATRIOTS!

The New England Patriots compete in the National Football **League's** (NFL's) American Football Conference (AFC). They play in the AFC East **division**, along with the Buffalo Bills, Miami Dolphins, and New York Jets. Fans of the Patriots have been lucky! The Patriots have played in more **Super Bowls** than any other team. The team is also tied for the most Super Bowl victories in NFL history with six. Let's learn more about the Patriots!

AFC EAST DIVISION

Buffalo Bills

Miami Dolphins

New England Patriots

New York Jets

TIGHT END HUNTER HENRY (RIGHT) JOINED THE PATRIOTS IN 2021 AFTER FIVE SEASONS WITH THE CHARGERS.

BROCK

BECOMING THE PATRIOTS

Originally called the Boston Patriots, the team was one of the original members of the American Football League (AFL). The team was named Patriots because Boston, Massachusetts, is considered the birthplace of the American Revolution. Patriots are people who make great efforts to support or defend their country. The team joined the NFL when the AFL and NFL combined in 1970. When the team moved from Boston to Foxborough, Massachusetts, they changed their name to the New England Patriots.

IN THEIR EARLIER YEARS, THE TEAM'S HELMETS INCLUDED AN IMAGE OF A PATRIOT HIKING THE FOOTBALL.

BY THE NUMBERS

The Patriots have won **SIX** Super Bowls.

11 straight playoff appearances from 2009 to 2019 for the Patriots

589 points scored by the team in 2007—a Patriots record!

16 wins for the Patriots in 2007

WIDE RECEIVER JULIAN EDELMAN WON THREE SUPER BOWLS AS A MEMBER OF THE PATRIOTS.

THE PATRIOTS HAVE MISSED THE PLAYOFFS ONLY THREE TIMES SINCE GILLETTE STADIUM OPENED IN 2002.

GAME DAY

Since 2002, the Patriots have played their home games at Gillette **Stadium**. Before that, the team played in Foxboro Stadium for more than 30 seasons. The stadium holds about 66,000 Patriots fans on game days. Amazingly, every game in Gillette Stadium's history has been a sellout, meaning fans purchased every available seat. In the first game ever played there, the Patriots defeated the Pittsburgh Steelers 30–14.

We're Famous!

During his 20 seasons with the team, quarterback Tom Brady was one of the most famous football players in the NFL. He even appeared as a cartoon version of himself on the hit FOX television show *The Simpsons*. In an episode from 2005, Brady attends a class taught by Homer Simpson.

UNIFORM

BLUE

WHITE

Truly Weird

During a 1982 home game against the Miami Dolphins, the entire field was covered with snow. No one scored for the game's first three quarters. In the fourth quarter, the Patriots had a chance for a 33-yard field goal. Their coach, Ron Meyer, had the brilliant idea to ask a team employee to use a snow plow on the spot where his kicker would attempt the kick. The field goal was good, and the Patriots won 3–0.

Alternate Jersey

Sometimes teams wear an alternate jersey that is different from their home and away jerseys. It might be a bright color or have a unique theme. The Patriots wore red jerseys and helmets with the old team logo for a 2012 game against the Jets. The different look proved lucky, as the Patriots won the game.

FANS AT GILLETTE STADIUM HAVE GROWN ACCUSTOMED TO WATCHING THE PATRIOTS SUCCEED ON THE FIELD.

TEAM SPIRIT

Going to a game at Gillette Stadium can be a ton of fun! After every Patriots **touchdown**, a group of people dressed as American Revolutionary soldiers pretend to fire their muskets, rifles from hundreds of years ago. The Patriots Cheerleaders entertain the fans at every game. They are joined by Pat Patriot, the team's mascot. He's a costumed American Revolutionary soldier wearing a Patriots jersey. Fans who come to the game hungry have plenty of options. Try the BBQ street tacos at Backyard Barbeque or a steak and cheese sub at the Tailgate Grill.

PAT PATRIOT

HEROES OF HISTORY

Rob Gronkowski

Tight End | 2010–2018

Gronkowski played nine seasons in New England. During that time, he helped lead the team to three Super Bowl victories. Gronkowski's 17 touchdown catches in 2011 are the most ever by a tight end in a single season. He has been chosen for five **Pro Bowls**.

John Hannah

Offensive Guard | 1973–1985

Hannah is considered one of the greatest offensive lineman of all time. He started every one of the 183 games he played in his career. He was chosen for the Pro Bowl nine times. Hannah was inducted into the Pro Football **Hall of Fame** in 1991.

Ty Law

Cornerback | 1995–2004

Law helped lead the Patriots to three Super Bowl wins. His 36 interceptions while in New England are tied for the most in team history. Law is tied for 12th all-time with seven interceptions returned for a touchdown. He was inducted into the Pro Football Hall of Fame in 2019.

Randy Moss

Wide Receiver | 2007–2010

Although he only played three full seasons for the Patriots, Moss made a major impact during his time in New England. As a Patriot, he twice led the NFL in touchdown catches. His 23 touchdown catches in 2007 are the most by a player in a single season in NFL history.

The Patriots defeat the Miami Dolphins 31–14 in the AFC Championship Game to earn their first-ever trip to the Super Bowl.

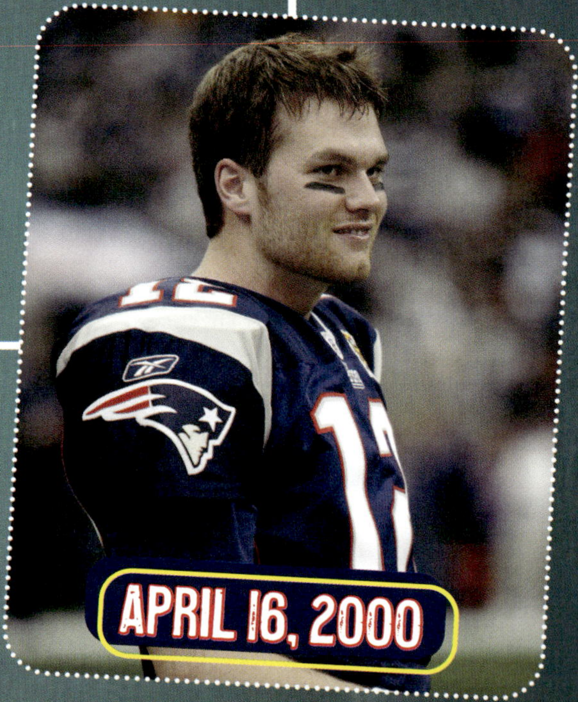

In the sixth round of the NFL Draft, New England selects University of Michigan quarterback Tom Brady.

BIG DAYS

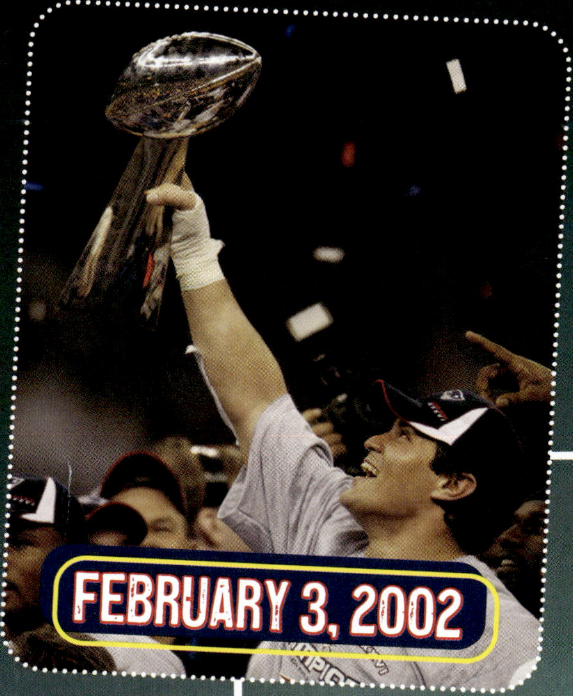

FEBRUARY 3, 2002

The Patriots defeat the St. Louis Rams 20–17 for the first Super Bowl in franchise history.

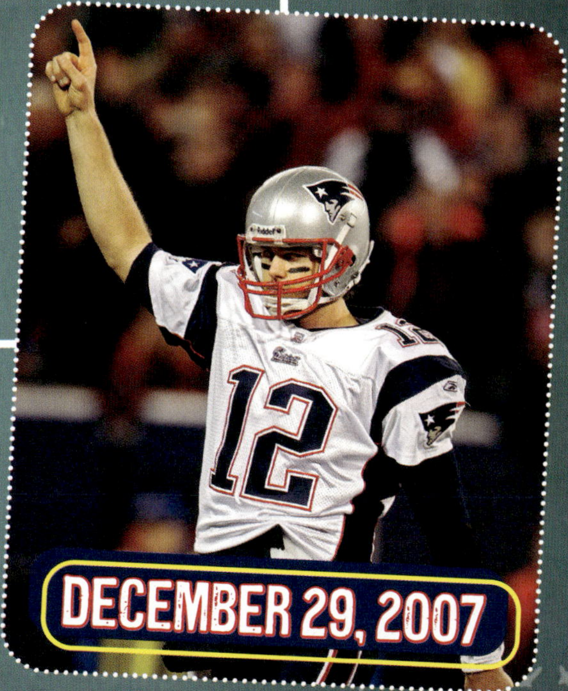

DECEMBER 29, 2007

The Patriots finish the second perfect regular season in NFL history, ending the season with a 16–0 record after defeating the New York Giants 38–35.

MODERN-DAY MARVELS

Damien Harris

Running Back | Debut: 2019

After starring at the University of Alabama, Harris was chosen by the Patriots in the third round of the 2019 NFL Draft. He led the team with 929 rushing yards in 2021. Harris also finished 2021 second in the NFL with 15 rushing touchdowns.

Dont'a Hightower

Linebacker | Debut: 2012

Hightower helped anchor Patriots' defenses that won three Super Bowls. Coach Bill Belichick referred to him as "Mr. February" because of the key plays he made in Super Bowls 49 and 51. Hightower has been chosen for the Pro Bowl twice.

Mac Jones

Mac Jones | Debut: 2021

The Patriots picked Jones 15th overall in the 2021 NFL Draft. He became the first Patriots **rookie** to start the first game of a season in more than 25 years. After leading the Patriots to a 10–7 record as a rookie, Jones was selected for the 2021 Pro Bowl.

DeVante Parker

Wide Receiver | Debut: 2022

Parker played his first seven seasons for the Miami Dolphins. He was traded to the Patriots before the 2022 season. Through 2021, Parker gained 4,727 receiving yards and caught 24 touchdown passes. He finished fifth in the NFL with 1,202 receiving yards in 2019. Parker is shown here in his old Dolphins uniform.

TOM BRADY STARTED 283 REGULAR SEASON GAMES FOR THE PATRIOTS.

THE GOAT

GREATEST OF ALL TIME

TOM BRADY

Considered by some to be the greatest player in NFL history, Brady led the Patriots to six Super Bowl victories. He played 20 seasons in New England. Brady won the league's **Most Valuable Player** (MVP) Award three times. Along with holding many other records, he is the NFL's all-time leader in passing yards and passing touchdowns. Brady has been chosen for 15 Pro Bowls as well as the NFL's 100th Anniversary All-Time Team.

FAN FAVORITE

Julian Edelman–Wide Receiver

2009–2020

Edelman played 11 seasons for the Patriots. His 6,822 receiving yards are the fourth most in team history. Edelman became one of the franchise's most beloved players for his aggressive play. He is only 5 feet, 10 inches (178 cm) tall, which is small for a wide receiver. But fans loved the way he gave it his all every time he stepped onto the field.

THE BIG GAME

FEBRUARY 3, 2019 – SUPER BOWL 53

The Patriots had a chance to tie the NFL record with six Super Bowl victories in Super 52 but lost to the Philadelphia Eagles. They earned another chance the next year. Their opponent was the Los Angeles Rams. The teams were locked in a defensive struggle after three quarters with the score tied 3–3. Midway through the fourth quarter, the Patriots drove down the field and scored a touchdown. They won the game 13–3. After catching ten passes in the game for 141 receiving yards, wide receiver Julian Edelman was named the game's MVP.

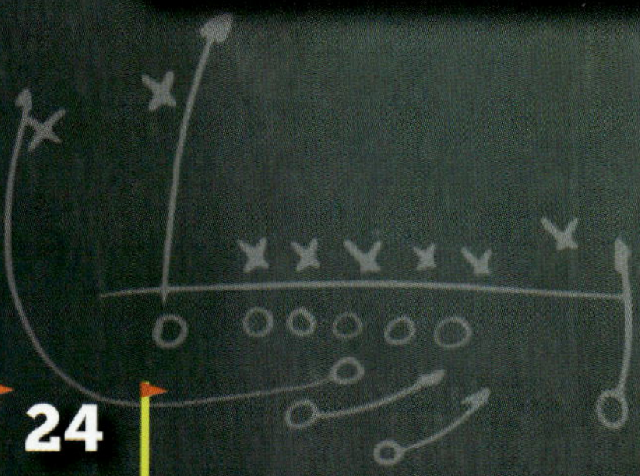

STRONG DEFENSES FOR BOTH TEAMS MADE SUPER BOWL 53 A LOW-SCORING GAME.

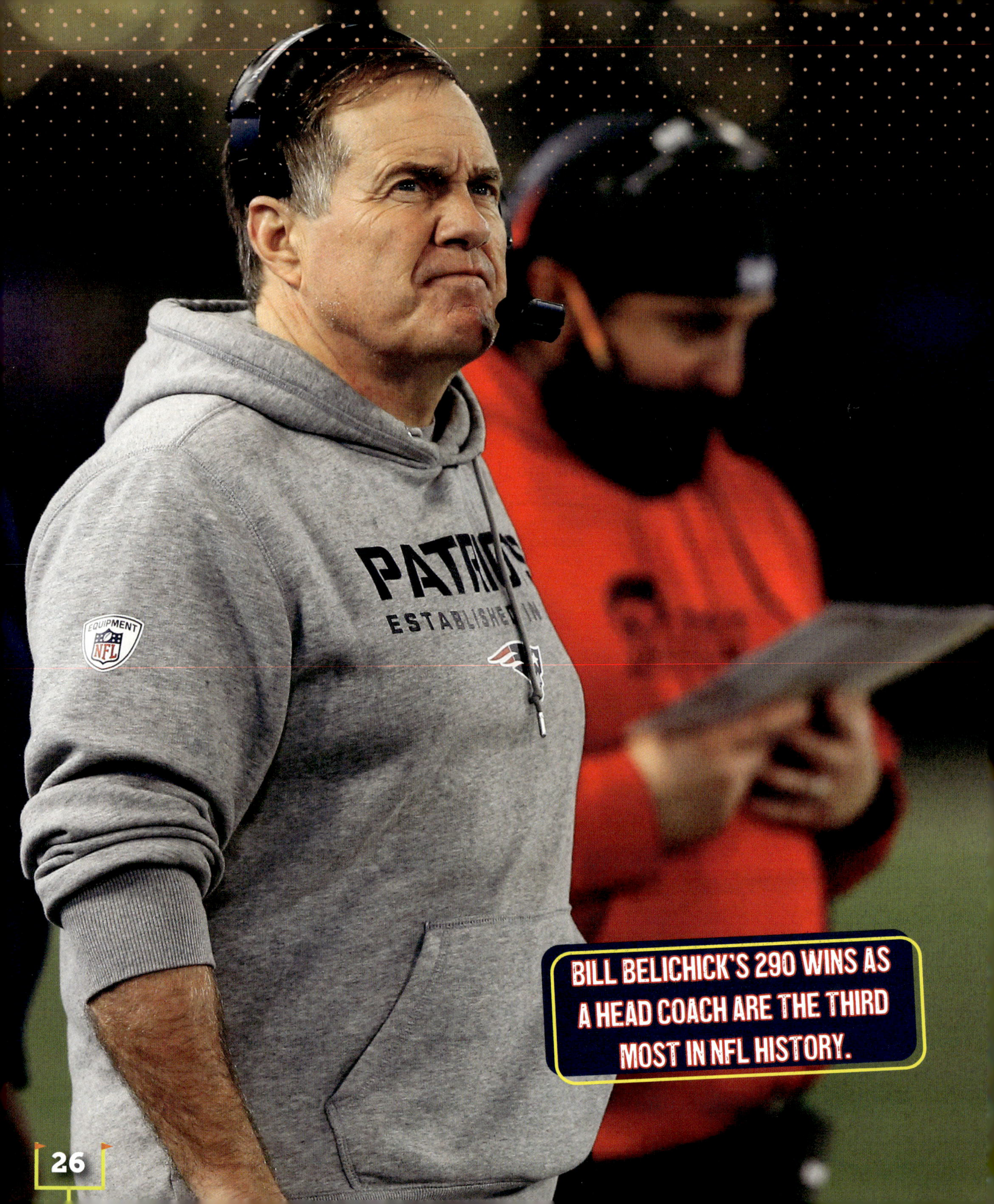

BILL BELICHICK'S 290 WINS AS A HEAD COACH ARE THE THIRD MOST IN NFL HISTORY.

AMAZING FEATS

50 Touchdown Passes

In 2007 by
QUARTERBACK
Tom Brady

18 Rushing Touchdowns

In 2016 by
RUNNING BACK
LeGarrette Blount

123 Catches

In 2009 by
WIDE RECEIVER
Wes Welker

18.5 Sacks

In 1984 by
LINEBACKER
Andre Tippett

ALL-TIME BEST

PASSING YARDS

Tom Brady
74,571
Drew Bledsoe
29,657
Steve Grogan
26,886

RUSHING YARDS

Sam Cunningham
5,543
Jim Nance
5,323
Tony Collins
4,647

RECEIVING YARDS

Stanley Morgan
10,352
Rob Gronkowski
7,861
Wes Walker
7,459

SACKS**

Andre Tippett
100
Julius Adams
80.5
Willie McGinest
78

SCORING

Stephen Gostkowski
1,775
Adam Vinatieri
1,158
Gino Cappelletti
1,130

INTERCEPTIONS

Raymond Clayborn
36
Ty Law
36
Devin McCourty
31*

*as of 2021
**unofficial before 1982

DREW BLEDSOE LED THE PATRIOTS TO THE SUPER BOWL AFTER THE 1996 SEASON.

GLOSSARY

division (dih-VIZSH-un): a group of teams within the NFL who play each other more frequently and compete for the best record

Hall of Fame (HAHL of FAYM): a museum in Canton, Ohio, that honors the best players in NFL history

league (LEEG): an organization of sports teams that compete against each other

Most Valuable Player (MOHST VALL-yuh-bul PLAY-uhr): a yearly award given to the top player in the NFL

Pro Bowl (PRO BOWL): the NFL's All-Star game where the best players in the league compete

rookie (RUH-kee): a player playing in his first season

sack (SAK): when a quarterback is tackled behind the line of scrimmage before he can throw the ball

stadium (STAY-dee-uhm): a building with a field and seats for fans where teams play

Super Bowl (SOO-puhr BOWL): the championship game of the NFL, played between the winners of the AFC and the NFC

touchdown (TUTCH-down): a play in which the ball is brought into the other team's end zone, resulting in six points

FIND OUT MORE

IN THE LIBRARY

Bulgar, Beth and Mark Bechtel. *My First Book of Football.* New York, NY: Time Inc. Books, 2015.

Jacobs, Greg. *The Everything Kids' Football Book, 7th Edition*. Avon, MA: Adams Media, 2021.

Sports Illustrated Kids. *The Greatest Football Teams of All Time*. New York, NY: Time Inc. Books, 2018.

Wyner, Zach. *New England Patriots*. New York, NY: AV2, 2020.

ON THE WEB

Visit our website for links about the New England Patriots:
childsworld.com/links

Note to parents, teachers, and librarians: We routinely verify our web links to make sure they are safe and active sites. Encourage your readers to check them out!

INDEX

ABOUT THE AUTHOR

Josh Anderson has published over 50 books for children and young adults. His two boys are the greatest joys in his life. Hobbies include coaching his sons in youth basketball, no-holds-barred games of Apples to Apples, and taking long family walks. His favorite NFL team is a secret he'll never share!